Mysticism

for

Beginners

Also by Adam Zagajewski

Tremor: Selected Poems (1985)

Solidarity, Solitude (1990)

Canvas (1991)

Two Cities (1995)

Mysticism

for

Beginners

Adam

Zagajewski

●

Translated from the Polish

by Clare Cavanagh

Farrar, Straus and Giroux

New York

Farrar, Straus and Giroux
19 Union Square West, New York 10003

Distributed in Canada by Douglas & McIntyre Ltd.
Printed in the United States of America
Designed by Jonathan D. Lippincott
First edition, 1997

Library of Congress Cataloging-in-Publication Data
Zagajewski, Adam, 1945–
    [Poems. English. Selections]
    Mysticism for beginners / Adam Zagajewski ; translated from the
Polish by Clare Cavanagh. — 1st ed.
        p.   cm.
    ISBN 0-374-21765-3 (hc : alk. paper)
    1. Zagajewski, Adam, 1945–   —Translations into English.
I. Cavanagh, Clare.   II. Title.
PG7185.A32A23   1997
891.8'517—dc21   97-9097

Acknowledgment is made to the following publications in which some
of these poems first appeared: *The New Republic* ("Self-portrait," "Hous-
ton, 6 p.m.," and "Refugees"), *Conjunctions* ("The Room I Work In"), *2B*
("Elegy"), and *Doubletake* ("Holy Saturday in Paris," "A Quick Poem,"
"Chinese Poem," "Shell," "Mysticism for Beginners," and "Moment").

Many of these poems originally appeared in Polish in the volume *Ziemia
Ognista*, published by A5 in Poznan in 1994.

Contents

Mysticism

for

Beginners

A Quick Poem

I was listening to Gregorian chants
in a speeding car
on a highway in France.
The trees rushed past. Monks' voices
sang praises to an unseen God
(at dawn, in a chapel trembling with cold).
Domine, exaudi orationem meam,
male voices pleaded calmly
as if salvation were just growing in the garden.
Where was I going? Where was the sun hiding?
My life lay tattered
on both sides of the road, brittle as a paper map.
With the sweet monks
I made my way toward the clouds, deep blue,
heavy, dense,
toward the future, the abyss,
gulping hard tears of hail.
Far from dawn. Far from home.
In place of walls—sheet metal.
Instead of a vigil—a flight.
Travel instead of remembrance.
A quick poem instead of a hymn.
A small, tired star raced
up ahead
and the highway's asphalt shone,
showing where the earth was,
where the horizon's razor lay in wait,
and the black spider of evening
and night, widow of so many dreams.

Transformation

I haven't written a single poem
in months.
I've lived humbly, reading the paper,
pondering the riddle of power
and the reasons for obedience.
I've watched sunsets
(crimson, anxious),
I've heard the birds grow quiet
and night's muteness.
I've seen sunflowers dangling
their heads at dusk, as if a careless hangman
had gone strolling through the gardens.
September's sweet dust gathered
on the windowsill and lizards
hid in the bends of walls.
I've taken long walks,
craving one thing only:
lightning,
transformation,
you.

September

—For Petr Král

I was in Prague looking for Vladimir Holan's house,
the prison-house where he spent fifteen years.
(I thought I'd find it easily, roosters
would guide me and an old priest
in a neatly mended cassock would say:
here lived the poet, and suffering slept here
like a stray cat, hiding once a week
in a fur coat's sleeve.)
                    The light already felt like fall,
the sun was a bit offended. September kissed the hills
and treetops like someone leaving
on a long trip who realizes only at the station
that he's lost his keys.
Inside the labyrinth tourists moved warily,
consulting the black void of their cameras.
The elms' flames floated over parks
like Saint Elmo's fire. Bonfires in gardens
and gray smoke above the earth, the wells.
But chestnut leaves, light and dry,
like a certain kind of unconcerned old age,
kept sailing higher.
What are baroque churches? Deluxe
health clubs for athletic saints.
They didn't want to help me. (Whoever seeks another's home,
one handsome, learnèd angel whispered,
will never find his own.) No one would help me.
Children shrieked happily
for no reason (full of cruelty just in case).
The wind was full of air, the air full of oxygen,
the oxygen held memories of a trip beyond the sea.
Was I right, were the palaces' walls, yellowed
as from nicotine, absorbed in border disputes?
I couldn't find Holan's house.
Life triumphed, as always, but the dead poet

dwelled in oblivion, in the sparks shooting
from beneath the welder's palm, in my growing exhaustion.
Nowhere, nowhere, nowhere at all.
He comes here, but only at night,
someone finally told me who wasn't there.

Mysticism for Beginners

The day was mild, the light was generous.
The German on the café terrace
held a small book on his lap.
I caught sight of the title:
Mysticism for Beginners.
Suddenly I understood that the swallows
patrolling the streets of Montepulciano
with their shrill whistles,
and the hushed talk of timid travelers
from Eastern, so-called Central Europe,
and the white herons standing—yesterday? the day before?—
like nuns in fields of rice,
and the dusk, slow and systematic,
erasing the outlines of medieval houses,
and olive trees on little hills,
abandoned to the wind and heat,
and the head of the *Unknown Princess*
that I saw and admired in the Louvre,
and stained-glass windows like butterfly wings
sprinkled with pollen,
and the little nightingale practicing
its speech beside the highway,
and any journey, any kind of trip,
are only mysticism for beginners,
the elementary course, prelude
to a test that's been
postponed.

Anthology

That evening I was reading an anthology.
Scarlet clouds grazed outside my window.
The spent day fled to a museum.

And you—who are you?
I don't know. I didn't know
if I was born for gladness?
Sorrow? Patient waiting?

In dusk's pure air
I read an anthology.
Ancient poets lived in me, singing.

The Three Kings

We'll arrive too late . . .
—*André Frénaud,* "The Three Kings"

If it hadn't been for the desert and laughter and music—
we'd have made it, if our yearning
hadn't mingled with the highways' dust.
We saw poor countries, made still poorer
by their ancient hatred;
a train full of soldiers and refugees
stood waiting at a burning station.
We were heaped with great honors
so we thought—perhaps one of us
really is a king?
Spring meadows detained us, cowslips,
the glances of country maidens
hungry for a stranger's love.
We made offerings to the gods, but we don't know
if they recognized our faces
through the flame's honey-gold veil.
Once we fell asleep and slept for many months,
but dreams raged in us, heavy, treacherous,
like surf beneath a full moon.
Fear awakened us and again we moved on,
cursing fate and filthy inns.
For four years a cold wind blew,
but the star was yellow, sewn carelessly to a coat
like a school insignia.
The taxi smelled of anise and the twentieth century,
the driver had a Russian accent.
Our ship sank, the plane shook suddenly.
We quarreled violently and each of us
set out in search of a different hope.
I barely remember what we were looking for
and I'm not sure if a December night
will open up someday

like a camera's eye.
Perhaps I'd be happy, live content,
if it weren't for the light that explodes
above the city walls each day
at dawn, blinding my desire.

The Greenhouse

In a small black town, your town,
where even trains linger unwilling,
anxious to be on their way,
in a park, defying soot and shadows,
a gray building stands lined with mother-of-pearl.

Forget the snow, the frost's repeated blows;
inside you're greeted by a damp anthology of breezes
and the enigmatic whispers of vast leaves
coiled like lazy snakes. Even an Egyptologist
couldn't make them out.

Forget the sadness of dark stadiums and streets,
the weight of thwarted Sundays.
Accept the warm breath wafting from the plants.
The gentle scent of faded lightning
engulfs you, beckoning you on.

Perhaps you see the rusty sails of ships at port,
islands snared in rosy mist, crumbling temples' towers;
you glimpse what you've lost, what never was,
and people with lives
like your own.

Suddenly you see the world lit differently,
other people's doors swing open for a moment,
you read their hidden thoughts, their holidays don't hurt,
their happiness is less opaque, their faces
almost beautiful.

Lose yourself, go blind from ecstasy,
forgetting everything, and then perhaps
a deeper memory, a deeper recognition will return,
and you'll hear yourself saying: I don't know how—
the palm trees opened up my greedy heart.

Dutch Painters

Pewter bowls heavy and swelling with metal.
Plump windows bulging from the light.
The palpability of leaden clouds.
Gowns like quilts. Moist oysters.
These things are immortal, but don't serve us.
The clogs walk by themselves.
The floor tiles are never bored,
and sometimes play chess with the moon.
An ugly girl studies a letter
written in invisible ink.
Is it about love or money?
The tablecloths smell of starch and morals.
The surface and depths don't connect.
Mystery? There's no mystery here, just blue sky,
restless and hospitable like a seagull's cry.
A woman neatly peeling a red apple.
Children dream of old age.
Someone reads a book (a book is read),
someone sleeps, becoming a warm object
that breathes like an accordion.
They liked dwelling. They dwelt everywhere,
in a wooden chair back,
in a milky streamlet narrow as the Bering Straits.
Doors were wide open, the wind was friendly.
Brooms rested after work well done.
Homes bared all. The painting of a land
without secret police.
Only on the young Rembrandt's face
an early shadow fell. Why?
Tell us, Dutch painters, what will happen
when the apple is peeled, when the silk dims,
when all the colors grow cold.
Tell us what darkness is.

Postcards

The asters burn with the dim glow
of velvet ribbons.
Then the chrysanthemums,
a faded northern shade of yellow.

It was All Saints' Day
but we had nowhere to go.
Our dead don't dwell in this country,
they pitch their tents in other dead men's memories,
in the fruits of hawthorn and lead.

It had been raining for a week, raindrops
marched into the earth
like Chinese warriors with rigid faces.
Mountain streams lay on their backs
greedily lapping up water and October,
and the clay shaped
ever more perfect forms.

We had nowhere to go
although the day was empty
like a sleeve buoyed by the wind.
Cemeteries swarmed with elegant,
unseen guests,
like a ballroom at dawn
when dreams pale.

Our dead don't live in this country—
they've been traveling for years.
The address they give on yellowed postcards
can't be read, and the nations engraved
on the stamps have long since ceased to exist.

The dictator could barely squeeze
onto the TV screen.
Parachutes blossomed in the sky
like forget-me-nots.
Say farewell, base days.
The ancient totems depart.
Uremia of justice.

Shell

At night the monks sang softly
and a gusting wind lifted
spruce branches like wings.
I've never visited the ancient cities,
I've never been to Thebes
or Delphi, and I don't know
what the oracles once told travelers.
Snow filled the streets and canyons,
and crows in dark robes silently
trailed the fox's footprints.
I believed in elusive signs,
in shadowed ruins, water snakes,
mountain springs, prophetic birds.
Linden trees bloomed like brides
but their fruit was small and bitter.
Wisdom can't be found
in music or fine paintings,
in great deeds, courage,
even love,
but only in all these things,
in earth and air, in pain and silence.
A poem may hold the thunder's echo,
like a shell touched by Orpheus
as he fled. Time takes life away
and gives us memory, gold with flame,
black with embers.

Iron Train

The train stopped at a little station
and for a moment stood absolutely still.
The doors slammed, gravel crunched underfoot,
someone said goodbye forever,

a glove dropped, the sun dimmed,
the doors slammed again, even louder,
and the iron train set off slowly
and vanished in the fog like the nineteenth century.

The Thirties

The thirties
I don't exist yet
Grass grows
A girl eats strawberry ice cream
Someone listens to Schumann
(mad, ruined
Schumann)
I don't exist yet
How fortunate
I can hear everything

Search

I returned to the town
where I was a child
and a teenager and an old man of thirty.
The town greeted me indifferently
but the streets' loudspeakers whispered:
don't you see the fire is still burning,
don't you hear the flame's roar?
Get out.
Find another place.
Search for it.
Search for your true homeland.

Referendum

Ukraine held a referendum
on independence.
It was foggy in Paris, the weatherman
predicted a cold and cloudy day.
I was angry at myself, at my
narrow, fettered life.
The Seine was trapped between embankment walls.
Bookstores showcased
a new edition of Schopenhauer's
Douleurs du monde.
Parisians wandered through the city
hidden in warm loden coats.
Fog infiltrated lips and lungs
as if the air were sobbing,
going on about itself, about the cold dawn,
how long the night is,
and how ruthless stars can be.
I took a bus toward the Bastille,
razed two hundred years ago,
and tried to read poems
but didn't understand a thing.

What comes after will be invisible
and easy.
Whatever is hesitates between irony
and fear.
Whatever survives will be blue
as a guillotine's eye.

Refugees

Bent under burdens which sometimes
can be seen and sometimes can't,
they trudge through mud or desert sands,
hunched, hungry,

silent men in heavy jackets,
dressed for all four seasons,
old women with crumpled faces,
clutching something—a child, the family
lamp, the last loaf of bread?

It could be Bosnia today,
Poland in September '39, France
eight months later, Germany in '45,
Somalia, Afghanistan, Egypt.

There's always a wagon or at least a wheelbarrow
full of treasures (a quilt, a silver cup,
the fading scent of home),
a car out of gas marooned in a ditch,
a horse (soon left behind), snow, a lot of snow,
too much snow, too much sun, too much rain,

and always that special slouch
as if leaning toward another, better planet,
with less ambitious generals,
less snow, less wind, fewer cannons,
less History (alas, there's no
such planet, just that slouch).

Shuffling their feet,
they move slowly, very slowly
toward the country of nowhere,
and the city of no one
on the river of never.

Letter from a Reader

Too much about death,
too many shadows.
Write about life,
an average day,
the yearning for order.

Take the school bell
as your model
of moderation,
even scholarship.

Too much death,
too much
dark radiance.

Take a look,
crowds packed
in cramped stadiums
sing hymns of hatred.

Too much music,
too little harmony, peace,
reason.

Write about those moments
when friendship's footbridges
seem more enduring
than despair.

Write about love,
long evenings,
the dawn,
the trees,
about the endless patience
of the light.

I Wasn't in This Poem

I wasn't in this poem,
only gleaming pure pools,
a lizard's tiny eye, the wind
and the sounds of a harmonica
pressed to not my lips.

For M.

I lay beneath the stars of another sky
in the black grass at midnight.
Midnight breathed, slow and lazy,
and I thought about you, about us,
about sharp and shining moments
plucked from my imagination like a thorn
drawn from an athlete's narrow foot.
That day the sea grew dark and
grim, the storm's orchids rushed
over crumpled sheets of water.
It could also have been childhood,
the land of easy ecstasy and endless longing,
red poppies in the lips of noon
and church towers alert as hummingbirds.
Soldiers walked along the street, but the war
was already over and rifles bloomed.
Some days the hush was so devout
we were afraid to move. A fox dashed across a field.
We tried the taste of leaves, the taste of light
that dazzles the innocent.
But the air had a bitter taste: carnations,
cinnamon, dust, and acorns,
winter, the first week of fall.
The bitter taste of unshed blood.
We stood a long time on the viaduct over the tracks
and a train must have passed under us;
only the dry sun was reflected
in its countless windows.
That's laughter, you said, that's iron,
salt, sand, glass.
                    And the future,
the fabric of your dress, life, which we shared
like a meal while traveling.

Far from Home

That morning the sky was veiled, dark
—clouds with enigmatic
Oriental faces
were in no hurry.
At noon the long blades of sunbeams
started pacing the city's rooftops
like scissors seeking victims.
Bonfires flared, smoke bowed to its masters,
while blood—the great absentee—
intoned its Gregorian chant.

That's Sicily

At night we sailed past shadowed,
enigmatic shores. Far off, the huge leaves
of hills swayed like a giant's dreams.
Waves slapped the boat's wood,
a warm wind kissed the sails,
stars rushed, helter-skelter,
to tell the history of the world.
That's Sicily, someone whispered,
three-cornered island, owl's breath,
handkerchief of the dead.

You Are My Silent Brethren

You are my silent brethren,
the dead.
I won't forget you.

In old letters I find traces of your writing,
creeping to the page's top
like a snail on the wall of a psychiatric ward.

Your addresses and phone numbers pitch camp
in my notebooks, waiting, dozing.

I was in Paris yesterday, I saw hundreds of tourists,
tired and cold. I thought, they look
like you, they can't get settled, they circle restlessly.

You'd think it would be easy, living.
All you need is a fistful of earth, a boat, a nest, a jail,
a little breath, some drops of blood, and longing.

You are my masters,
the dead.
Don't forget me.

Out Walking

Sometimes out walking, on a country road
or in a quiet green forest,
you hear scraps of voices, perhaps they're calling you,
you don't want to believe them, you walk faster,
but they catch up quickly,
like tame animals.

You don't want to believe them, then later
on a busy city street
you're sorry you didn't listen
and you try to summon up
the syllables, the sounds, and the intervals between them.

But it's too late now
and you'll never know
who was singing, which song,
and where it was drawing you.

Whatever Happened

Whatever happened had already happened.
Four tons of death lie on the grass
and dry tears endure among the herbarium's leaves.
Whatever happened will stay with us
and with us will grow and diminish.

But we must live,
the rusting chestnut tells us.
We must live,
the locust sings.
We must live,
the hangman whispers.

Vermeer's Little Girl

Vermeer's little girl, now famous,
watches me. A pearl watches me.
The lips of Vermeer's little girl
are red, moist, and shining.

Oh Vermeer's little girl, oh pearl,
blue turban: you are all light
and I am made of shadow.
Light looks down on shadow
with forbearance, perhaps pity.

Cicadas

The hawk, a little lost,
I thought,
circled over an azure sea.
The cliffs warmed and grew.
We swam a long time, buried in the water.
A minibus dropped off mongoloid children
with pale faces
like unfinished marble statues.
My skin tasted salty,
I'd become a rock, a mineral.
We read our hot books lazily.
Resin melted in the pines.
We exist between the elements,
between fire and sleep.
Pain chases
or outstrips us.

Tierra del Fuego

You who see our homes at night
and the frail walls of our conscience,
you who hear our conversations
droning on like sewing machines
—save me, tear me from sleep,
from amnesia.

Why is childhood—oh, tinfoil treasures,
oh, the rustling of lead, lovely and foreboding—
our only origin, our only longing?
Why is manhood, which takes the place of ripeness,
an endless highway,
Sahara yellow?

After all, you know there are days
when even thirst runs dry
and prayer's lips harden.

Sometimes the sun's coin dims
and life shrinks so small
that you could tuck it
in the blue gloves of the Gypsy
who predicts the future
for seven generations back

and then in some other little town
in the south a charlatan
decides to destroy you,
me, and himself.

You who see the whites of our eyes,
you who hide like a bullfinch
in the rowans,
like a falcon
in the clouds' warm stockings

—open the boxes full of song,
open the blood that pulses in aortas
of animals and stones,
light lanterns in black gardens.

Nameless, unseen, silent,
save me from anesthesia,
take me to Tierra del Fuego,
take me where the rivers
flow straight up, horizontal rivers
flowing up and down.

Albi

The traveler greets his new setting,
hoping to find happiness there,
perhaps even his memory.

Albi opens before me—
an acacia leaf, soft and friendly

—but the basilica can't be vanquished,
its slick walls and dagger windows
deflect my emotions.

A west wind blows, from Spain,
bearing a drop of sorrow and an atom of ocean.
Plane trees greet each other
like courtiers in green gowns
dusty from a long carriage ride.

I still don't know what the world is,
a tall wave drowning the senses,
courage and peace and the still flames of lanterns
tonight as we bid the dead farewell;

fatigue and fertile dreams
pass through us like relentless pilgrims.

The patient basilica stands still.
Clouds swim, sleepy, lazy,
like a lowland river.
The fire-archer poises over me, fixed and shifting.

You're no longer here,
but I'm alive, alive and looking,
and the ball of my breath
rolls through narrow country roads.

Flags

Flags, overcoats, where nations
bivouac, tired, black with exhaustion,
flags, the crumpled sheets of heroes,
flags, stop shielding our eyes,

go back to the cotton fields,
go back to Asia.
Don't you know
that night is coming
and a tornado of stars
and the sequins grow uneasy?

Self-portrait

Between the computer, a pencil, and a typewriter
half my day passes. One day it will be half a century.
I live in strange cities and sometimes talk
with strangers about matters strange to me.
I listen to music a lot: Bach, Mahler, Chopin, Shostakovich.
I see three elements in music: weakness, power, and pain.
The fourth has no name.
I read poets, living and dead, who teach me
tenacity, faith, and pride. I try to understand
the great philosophers—but usually catch just
scraps of their precious thoughts.
I like to take long walks on Paris streets
and watch my fellow creatures, quickened by envy,
anger, desire; to trace a silver coin
passing from hand to hand as it slowly
loses its round shape (the emperor's profile is erased).
Beside me trees expressing nothing
but a green, indifferent perfection.
Black birds pace the fields,
waiting patiently like Spanish widows.
I'm no longer young, but someone else is always older.
I like deep sleep, when I cease to exist,
and fast bike rides on country roads when poplars and houses
dissolve like cumuli on sunny days.
Sometimes in museums the paintings speak to me
and irony suddenly vanishes.
I love gazing at my wife's face.
Every Sunday I call my father.
Every other week I meet with friends,
thus proving my fidelity.
My country freed itself from one evil. I wish
another liberation would follow.
Could I help in this? I don't know.
I'm truly not a child of the ocean,

as Antonio Machado wrote about himself,
but a child of air, mint, and cello
and not all the ways of the high world
cross paths with the life that—so far—
belongs to me.

December Wind

The December wind kills hope,
but don't let it take
the blue mist from the ocean
and the summer morning's mildness.

Who believes that invisible,
light islands still exist
and stains of sunshine
on a parquet floor?

Sleep wanders in rags
begging for alms
while memory, like Mary Stuart,
withers in a prison cell.

Traveler

A certain traveler, who believed in nothing,
found himself one summer in a foreign city.
Lindens were blossoming, and foreignness bloomed devoutly.

An unknown crowd walked down the fragrant boulevard,
slowly, full of fear, perhaps because
the setting sun weighed more than the horizon

and the asphalt's scarlet might not
just be shadows and the guillotine
might not grace museums alone

and church bells chiming in chorus
might mean more than they usually mean.
Perhaps that's why the traveler kept

putting his hand to his chest, checking warily
to make sure he still had his return ticket
to the ordinary places where we live.

The House

Do you still remember what the house was like?
The house—a pocket in a snowstorm's overcoat,
houses, low and bulging like Egyptian vowels.
Sheltered by green tongues of trees—
the most faithful was the linden, it shed
dry tears each fall.
Outmoded dresses dangled in the attic
like hanged men. Old letters flamed.
The old piano dozing in the parlor,
a hippo with black and yellow teeth.
On the wall a cross from a failed uprising
hung crookedly, and a photo
of a sad girl—a failed life.
The air smelled like vermouth,
bitter and sweet at once.
Houses, houses, where are you,
under what ocean, in what memory,
beneath the roof of what existence?
While the wind was opening windows, a deep blue
past sneaked into the rooms
and stifled the muslin curtains' breathing.
The fire was death's intended
and brought her bouquets of pale sparks.

Moment

In the Romanesque church round stones
that ground down so many prayers and generations
kept humble silence, and shadows slept in the apse
like bats in winter furs.

We went out. The pale sun shone,
tinny music tinkled softly
from a car, two jays
studied us, humans,
threads of longing dangled in the air.

The present moment is shameless,
taking its foolish liberties
beside the wall
of this tired old shrine,

awaiting the millions of years to come,
future wars, geological eras,
cease-fires, treaties, changes in climate—
this moment—what is it?—just

a mosquito, a fly, a speck, a scrap of breath,
and yet it's taken over everywhere,
entering the timid grass,
inhabiting stems and genes,
the pupils of our eyes.

This moment, mortal as you or I,
was full of boundless, senseless,
silly joy, as if it knew
something we didn't.

Blackbird

A blackbird sat on the TV antenna
and sang a gentle, jazzy tune.
Whom have you lost, I asked, what do you mourn?
I'm taking leave of those who've gone, the blackbird said,
I'm parting with the day (its eyes and lashes),
I mourn a girl who lived in Thrace,
you wouldn't know her.
I'm sorry for the willow, killed by frost.
I weep, since all things pass and alter
and return, but always in a different form.
My narrow throat can barely hold
the grief, despair, delight, and pride
occasioned by such sweeping transformations.
A funeral cortege passes up ahead,
the same each evening, there, on the horizon's thread.
Everyone's there, I see them all and bid farewell.
I see the swords, hats, kerchiefs, and bare feet,
guns, blood, and ink. They walk slowly
and vanish in the river mist, on the right bank.
I say goodbye to them and you and the light,
and then I greet the night, since I serve her—
and black silks, black powers.

Elegy

It was a gray landscape, houses small
as Tartar ponies, concrete high-rises,
massive, stillborn; uniforms everywhere, rain,
drowsy rivers not knowing where to flow,
dust, Soviet gods with swollen eyelids,
sour smell of gas, sweet smell of tedium,
grimy trains, the red-eyed dawn.

It was a little landscape, endless winters,
in which there dwelled, as if in ancient lindens,
sparrows and knives and friendship and leaves of treason;
the arcs of village streets; pinched meadows; on a park bench
someone idly played the accordion
and for a moment you could breathe air
lighter than fatigue.

It was a waiting room with brown walls,
a courtroom, a clinic; a room
where tables slumped under files
and ashtrays choked on ashes.
It was silence or loudspeakers shrieking.
A waiting room where you waited
a lifetime to be born.

Our short-lived loves lasting so long,
our mighty laughter, ironies and triumphs
perhaps still fading in a police station
on the map's margin, on the edge of imagination.
The voices, the hair of the dead.
The chronometers of our desire,
a time full of emptiness.

It was a black landscape, only the mountains were blue
and a rainbow sloped. There were no promises, no hopes,
but we lived there, and not as strangers.

It was the life we'd been given.
It was patience, glacier-pale.
It was fear full of guilt. Courage
full of anxiety. Anxiety filled with power.

My train chugs along a ruddy meadow,
where a traveling circus has pitched camp.
Acrobats in pink shirts
are playing soccer; the tiger yawns.
The Seine flows north, carried along
by barges, ships, and motorboats.
A huge cloud screens the sky briefly.
But the swallows are already taking leave
of autumn, they chat awhile with the wind
and the Judas tree, who's feeling down.
The four elements doze and wake.
Who knows, behind the dark cloud
a small star may be playing.
I'm going to see my friend, my master.
My friend's memory is fading.
Its place is taken by knowledge
light as a spring at night.

Robespierre Before the Mirror

I have thin lips and a sharp nose.
There's something austere about my face.
My gaze is stern
and implacable.
Historians of our great revolution
will surely describe me this way.
"Ruthless, implacable, ambitious."
I myself can't know who I am,
but now, at dawn, in June,
in the village where I stand before a mirror
rosy from the rising sun,
I perceive in my face the smile
and softness
one usually associates
with sentiment and weakness.
On my left cheek I bear a black cloud.

Cello

Those who don't like it say it's
just a mutant violin
that's been kicked out of the chorus.
Not so.
The cello has many secrets,
but it never sobs,
just sings in its low voice.
Not everything turns into song
though. Sometimes you catch
a murmur or a whisper:
I'm lonely,
I can't sleep.

The hats are innocent, bathed
in a soft light blurring their forms.
The girl is hard at work.
But where are the brooks? The groves?
Where's the sensuous laughter of nymphs?
The world is hungry, and one day
it will invade this peaceful room.
For the time being it's appeased by ambassadors
announcing: I'm ocher.
And I'm sienna. I'm the color of terror,
like ash. Ships drown in me.
I'm the color blue, I'm cold,
I can be ruthless.
And I'm the color of death,
I'm endlessly patient.
I'm purple (you can barely see me),
triumphs and parades are mine.
I'm green, I'm tender,
I live in wells and birch leaves.
The girl, with her deft fingers,
doesn't hear the voices, since she's mortal.
She thinks about next Sunday,
and her date with the butcher's son
who has thick lips
and big hands
stained with blood.

Planetarium

Let's say it was September.
An artificial sky revolved above us.
Us, the school class. Me, my eyes,
my easy life, my sixteen years.
On the ceiling stars like dancers
made appearances, comets hurried
on their errands to the far ends of the earth.
The small explosions on the screen—
the loudspeaker explained—are in fact
terrifyingly vast, but essential
and predictable.
                    Let's suppose that for a second
the lights dimmed and darkness fell,
a black wind blew.
It seemed to be raining, hailing,
a thunderstorm approached, someone yelled
for help, begged the real
stars to return.
                    Let's say they came back
and their light was blinding.

She Wrote in Darkness

—To Ryszard Krynicki

While living in Stockholm Nelly Sachs
worked at night by a dim lamp,
so as not to waken her sick mother.

She wrote in darkness.
Despair dictated words
heavy as a comet's tail.

She wrote in darkness,
in silence broken only
by the wall clock's sighs.

Even the letters grew drowsy,
their heads drooping on the page.

Darkness wrote,
having taken this middle-aged woman
for its fountain pen.

Night took pity on her,
morning's gray prison
rose over the city,
rosy-fingered dawn.

While she dozed off
the blackbirds woke
and there was no break
in the sorrow and song.

Airport in Amsterdam

—In memory of my mother

December rose, pinched desire
in the dark and empty garden,
rust on the trees and thick smoke
as if someone's loneliness were burning.

Out walking yesterday I thought again
about the airport in Amsterdam—
the corridors without apartments,
waiting rooms filled with other people's dreams
stained with misfortune.

Airplanes struck the cement
almost angrily, hawks
without prey, hungry.

Maybe your funeral should have been held
here—hubbub, bustling crowds,
a good place not to be.

One has to look after the dead
beneath the airport's great tent.
We were nomads again;
you wandered westward in your summer dress,
amazed by war and time,
the moldering ruins, the mirror
reflecting a little, tired life.

In the darkness final things shone:
the horizon, a knife, and every rising sun.
I saw you off at the airport, hectic
valley where tears are for sale.

December rose, sweet orange:
without you there can be
no Christmases.

Mint leaves soothe a migraine . . .
In restaurants you always
studied the menu longest . . .
In our ascetic family
you were the mistress of expression,
but you died so quietly . . .

The old priest will garble your name.
The train will halt in the forest.
At dawn snow will fall
on the airport in Amsterdam.

Where are you?
There where memory lies buried.
There where memory grows.
There where the orange, rose, and snow lie buried.
There where ashes grow.

Night

Dances beautifully
and has great desires.
Seeks the road.
Weeps in the woods.
Is killed by dawn, fever,
and the rooster.

Long Afternoons

Those were the long afternoons when poetry left me.
The river flowed patiently, nudging lazy boats to sea.
Long afternoons, the coast of ivory.
Shadows lounged in the streets, haughty manikins in shopfronts
stared at me with bold and hostile eyes.

Professors left their schools with vacant faces,
as if the *Iliad* had finally done them in.
Evening papers brought disturbing news,
but nothing happened, no one hurried.
There was no one in the windows, you weren't there;
even nuns seemed ashamed of their lives.

Those were the long afternoons when poetry vanished
and I was left with the city's opaque demon,
like a poor traveler stranded outside the Gare du Nord
with his bulging suitcase wrapped in twine
and September's black rain falling.

Oh, tell me how to cure myself of irony, the gaze
that sees but doesn't penetrate; tell me how to cure myself
of silence.

To My Older Brother

How calmly we walk
through the days and months,
how softly we sing
our black lullaby,
how easily wolves seize
our brothers,
how gently
death breathes,
how swiftly
ships swim
in our arteries.

The City Where I Want to Live

The city is quiet at dusk,
when pale stars waken from their swoon,
and resounds at noon with the voices
of ambitious philosophers and merchants
bearing velvet from the East.
The flames of conversation burn there,
but not pyres.
Old churches, the mossy stones
of ancient prayer, are both its ballast
and its rocket ship.
It is a just city
where foreigners aren't punished,
a city quick to remember
and slow to forget,
tolerating poets, forgiving prophets
for their hopeless lack of humor.
The city was based
on Chopin's preludes,
taking from them only joy and sorrow.
Small hills circle it
in a wide collar; ash trees
grow there, and the slim poplar,
chief justice in the state of trees.
The swift river flowing through the city's heart
murmurs cryptic greetings
day and night
from the springs, the mountains, and the sky.

The Last Storm

Some are leaving.
Others drink silence.
Only storms shriek now in August
like a madman hauled off in an ambulance.
Branches beat our cheeks.
Alder leaves smell of sleep and straw oil.
You must listen, listen, listen.
Tired springs breathe under water.
At four in the morning
the last, lonely bolt of lightning
scribbles something quickly in the sky.
It says "No." Or "Never."
Or "Take courage, the fire's not dead."

Persephone

Persephone goes underground again
in a summer dress, with a Jewish
child's big eyes.

Kites fly, and yellow leaves, autumn dust,
a white plane, black crow wings.
Someone runs down the path clutching an overdue letter.

She'll be cold underground in cork
sandals and her hair won't shield
her from the blind wind, from oblivion—

she disappears into the chestnut trees
and only the ribbon on her braid
shines with resignation's rosy glow.

Persephone goes underground again
and again the same thread of indifference
binds my tiny bird-heart.

This Day's Nothingness

This day's nothingness
as if from spite
became a flame
and scorched the lips
of children and poets.

The Room I Work In

—*To Derek Walcott*

The room I work in is as foursquare
as half a pair of dice.
It holds a wooden table
with a stubborn peasant's profile,
a sluggish armchair, and a teapot's
pouting Hapsburg lip.
From the window I see a few skinny trees,
wispy clouds, and toddlers,
always happy and loud.
Sometimes a windshield glints in the distance
or, higher up, an airplane's silver husk.
Clearly others aren't wasting time
while I work, seeking adventures
on earth or in the air.
The room I work in is a camera obscura.
And what is my work—
waiting motionless,
flipping pages, patient meditation,
passivities not pleasing
to that judge with the greedy gaze.
I write as slowly as if I'll live two hundred years.
I seek images that don't exist,
and if they do they're crumpled and concealed
like summer clothes in winter,
when frost stings the mouth.
I dream of perfect concentration; if I found it
I'd surely stop breathing.
Maybe it's good I get so little done.
But after all, I hear the first snow hissing,
the frail melody of daylight,
and the city's gloomy rumble.
I drink from a small spring,
my thirst exceeds the ocean.

Three Angels

Suddenly three angels appeared
right here by the bakery on St. George Street.
Not another census bureau survey,
one tired man sighed.
No, the first angel said patiently,
we just wanted to see
what your lives have become,
the flavor of your days and why
your nights are marked by restlessness and fear.

That's right, fear, a lovely, dreamy-eyed
woman replied; but I know why.
The labors of the human mind have faltered.
They seek help and support
they can't find. Sir, just take a look
—she called the angel "Sir"!—
at Wittgenstein. Our sages
and leaders are melancholy madmen
and know even less than us
ordinary people (but she wasn't
ordinary).

            Then too, said one boy
who was learning to play the violin, evenings
are just an empty carton,
a casket minus mysteries,
while at dawn the cosmos seems as
parched and foreign as a TV screen.
And besides, those who love music for itself
are few and far between.

Others spoke up and their laments
surged into a swelling sonata of wrath.
If you gentlemen want to know the truth,
one tall student yelled—he'd

just lost his mother—we've had enough
of death and cruelty, persecution, disease,
and long spells of boredom still
as a serpent's eye. We've got too little earth
and too much fire. We don't know who we are.
We're lost in the forest, and black stars
move lazily above us as if
they were only our dream.

But still, the second angel mumbled shyly,
there's always a little joy, and even beauty
lies close at hand, beneath the bark
of every hour, in the quiet heart of concentration,
and another person hides in each of us—
universal, strong, invincible.
Wild roses sometimes hold the scent
of childhood, and on holidays young girls
go out walking just as they always have,
and there's something timeless
in the way they wind their scarves.
Memory lives in the ocean, in galloping blood,
in black, burnt stones, in poems,
and in every quiet conversation.
The world is the same as it always was,
full of shadows and anticipation.

He would have gone on talking, but the crowd
was growing larger and waves
of mute rage spread
until at last the envoys rose lightly
into the air, whence, growing distant,
they gently repeated: peace be unto you,
peace to the living, the dead, the unborn.
The third angel alone said nothing,
for that was the angel of long silence.

From Memory

The narrow street rears up from memory—
let it be this poem's larynx—
and the thick gray smoke above the coking plant,
casting sparks into the sky like a volcano,
repaying its debt to the stars.

My street: two proud old maids
with narrow lips—they'd survived Siberia
and Stalin; a young actor, craving fame,
and Professor G., who'd lost an arm in the Uprising
and wore his empty shirtsleeve like a sail.

I don't know anything yet, nothing's happened,
not counting the war or the massacre of Jews.
In winter gray snow lurks on rooftops,
alert as an Indian, dreading spring.
Vacation comes, a peeled orange.

A greedy priest gulps Gospels
in the crimson, Neo-Gothic church;
oh, heart of hearts, Christ's wounded breast.
Thank God for cream puffs after Mass
to help erase your Latin tortures.

In the barracks new recruits are training,
one of my friends plays the trumpet
like Miles Davis, only better.
Young ladies promenade
in wide starched skirts.

The ugly earth, gashed by flat
black rivers, scarred
like a German student's cheek,
held still all day; at night
it crooned in two languages,

and we also lived in two idioms,
in the cramped jargon of the commonplace, of envy,
and in the language of a great dream.
At noon the clouds' eye gently
opened, the eye of tears and light.

Summer

That summer was so hot and muggy . . .
The white sky hung above me like a circus tent.
I talked to myself, wrote letters,
dialed interminable numbers.
It was so stifling that ink
dried up in fountain pens. Hawks swooned.
I even sent a telegram, accepted
with a start by the dozing post office.
Drunken wasps reeled above the table,
sugar cubes burst in black coffee.
I wandered through the town and turned
slightly invisible, out of habit,
from despair. I talked to myself.
An airport, a train station, a church
shot up at the end of every street.
Travelers spoke of fires and omens.
I looked for you everywhere, everywhere.
Shutters were locked, borders sealed,
only clouds stole westward.
It was so hot, the lead dripped
from stained-glass windows.

Chinese Poem

I read a Chinese poem
written a thousand years ago.
The author talks about the rain
that fell all night
on the bamboo roof of his boat
and the peace that finally
settled in his heart.
Is it just coincidence
that it's November again, with fog
and a leaden twilight?
Is it just chance
that someone else is living?
Poets attach great importance
to prizes and success
but autumn after autumn
tears leaves from the proud trees
and if anything remains
it's only the soft murmur of the rain
in poems
neither happy nor sad.
Only purity can't be seen,
and evening, when both light and shadow
forget us for a moment,
busily shuffling mysteries.

But maybe it's just
the feast day of spring rain:
boats cruise the gutters
with sails made of yesterday's paper,
otherwise known as *Le Monde*.
The butchers are about to rub their eyes,
and the city will awaken, sad and sated.
Someone once saw the earth split open
and swallow up a bit of future.
Luckily the rip was insignificant
and may still be stitched.
Some birds began to stammer.
Let's go someplace else, you say,
where monks sing
their songs poured from lead.
Alas, in the Arab quarter
a cloud, two-headed like the tsarist eagle,
bars the road.
And two-headed doubts,
slim as antelopes,
barricade the damp street.
Lord, why did you die?

On Swimming

The rivers of this country are sweet
as a troubador's song,
the heavy sun wanders westward
on yellow circus wagons.
Little village churches
hold a fabric of silence so fine
and old that even a breath
could tear it.
I love to swim in the sea, which keeps
talking to itself
in the monotone of a vagabond
who no longer recalls
exactly how long he's been on the road.
Swimming is like prayer:
palms join and part,
join and part,
almost without end.

Sisters of Mercy

That was childhood, which won't come back—
berries so black the night was envious;
slim poplars rose above the narrow river
like sisters of mercy and weren't afraid of strangers.
From the balcony I could see a little street and two trees,
but I was also the emperor and listened blissfully
as my countless armies roared
and the captured Turkish banners fluttered.

I liked the taste of grass between my teeth,
the bitter maple leaves, the sour sweetness
of June's first strawberry in my mouth.
Sunday morning Mother made real coffee,
in church the old priest waged war on pride.
My heart hurt whenever I saw someone poor.
Blue and yellow countries lived inside the atlas;
big nations swallowed up little ones, but on stamps

you just saw resting eagles, zebras,
giraffes, and tiny tomtits with their breathless grace.
On the dark shop's dusty shelves
jars of sticky candies towered.
Scarlet moths flew out when they were opened.
I was a Boy Scout and got to know loneliness
in the woods when dusk fell, the owl cried,
and the oak boughs creaked alarmingly.

I read stories about knights, Russian folktales,
and Sienkiewicz's unending trilogy.
My father built me a miniature mill,
which spun swiftly in the mountain stream.
My bike outran the panting locomotive,
August heat melted the gray city like ice cream.
Berries so black . . . bitter maple leaves . . .
That was childhood. Blood and feast days.

Houston, 6 p.m.

Europe already sleeps beneath a coarse plaid of borders
and ancient hatreds: France nestled
up to Germany, Bosnia in Serbia's arms,
lonely Sicily in azure seas.

It's early evening here, the lamp is lit
and the dark sun swiftly fades.
I'm alone, I read a little, think a little,
listen to a little music.

I'm where there's friendship,
but no friends, where enchantment
grows without magic,
where the dead laugh.

I'm alone because Europe is sleeping. My love
sleeps in a tall house on the outskirts of Paris.
In Krakow and Paris my friends
wade in the same river of oblivion.

I read and think; in one poem
I found the phrase "There are blows so terrible . . .
Don't ask!" I don't. A helicopter
breaks the evening quiet.

Poetry calls us to a higher life,
but what's low is just as eloquent,
more plangent than Indo-European,
stronger than my books and records.

There are no nightingales or blackbirds here
with their sad, sweet cantilenas,
only the mockingbird who imitates
and mimics every living voice.

Poetry summons us to life, to courage
in the face of the growing shadow.
Can you gaze calmly at the Earth
like the perfect astronaut?

Out of harmless indolence, the Greece of books,
and the Jerusalem of memory there suddenly appears
the island of a poem, unpeopled;
some new Cook will discover it one day.

Europe is already sleeping. Night's animals,
mournful and rapacious,
move in for the kill.
Soon America will be sleeping, too.

I walked through the medieval town
in the evening or at dawn,
I was very young or rather old.
I didn't have a watch
or a calendar, only my stubborn blood
measured the endless expanse.
I could begin life, mine
or not mine, over,
everything seemed easy,
apartment windows were partway open,
other fates ajar.
It was spring or early summer,
warm walls,
air soft as an orange rind;
I was very young or rather old,
I could choose, I could live.